Mysterious You

Hmm?

The most interesting book you'll ever read about memory

Written by Diane Swanson

Illustrated by Rose Cowles

Kids Can Press

Despite his grueling schedule, Dr. Barry Beyerstein, Brain Behavior Laboratory, Department of Psychology, Simon Fraser University, gave generously of his time and expertise to review and comment on this book. I appreciate his contribution beyond words. Thanks also to the many other scientists whose research gave me an insight into the mysterious world of memory. As well, my gratitude extends to my partners, editor Val Wyatt and illustrator Rose Cowles, for lending their considerable skills and talents to this project and to the British Columbia Arts Council for its support.

Kids Can Press acknowledges the financial support of the Ontario Arts Council, the Canada Council for the Arts and the Government of Canada, through the BPIDP, for our publishing activity.

Published in Canada by
Kids Can Press Ltd.
29 Birch Avenue
Toronto, ON M4V 1E2

Published in the U.S. by
Kids Can Press Ltd.
2250 Military Road
Tonawanda, NY 14150

Edited by Valerie Wyatt
Designed by Marie Bartholomew

Medical clip art on pages 6–7 from LifeART images © 1998 William & Wilkins. All rights reserved.

Printed in Hong Kong by Wing King Tong Company Limited

The hardcover edition of this book is smyth sewn casebound.
The paperback edition of this book is limp sewn with a drawn-on cover.

CM 01 0 9 8 7 6 5 4 3 2 1
CM PA 01 0 9 8 7 6 5 4 3 2 1

Canadian Cataloguing in Publication Data

Swanson, Diane, 1944–
        Hmm? : the most interesting book you'll ever read about memory

(Mysterious you)
Includes index.

ISBN 1-55074-595-6 (bound) ISBN 1-55074-597-2 (pbk.)

1. Memory — Juvenile literature. I. Cowles, Rose, 1967– .
II. Title. III. Series: Mysterious you (Toronto, Ont.).

QP7406.S92 2001 j612.8'2 C00-932222-1

Kids Can Press is a Nelvana company

Contents

Memory for Life

Imagine memorizing hundreds of meaningless syllables, such as sa, vo and ni. Now imagine reciting them in order — forward AND backward. Tough to do? You bet. But not for a Russian named Solomon-Veniaminovich Shereshevskii, known to scientists as "S." The researchers who studied his astounding memory discovered he could remember long lists of syllables in perfect order for at least 15 years! He could even recall when he was first given each list and what the scientist was wearing at the time.

It helped that S experienced synesthesia (sin-es-THEE-zha) — a rare overlapping of the senses. With every word he heard or read, he saw images. He often sensed textures or tastes, too. Some words appeared as puffs of steam; others felt prickly. The numeral "3" twirled and created an image of a gloomy person. So vivid were these sensations that S often remembered words and numbers without even trying.

You might think it would be great to have such a super memory, but S's memory made his life difficult. He recalled so many details of a face that he had trouble bringing them all together in a single image. He was so distracted by the memories of countless everyday events that he found it hard to keep a job. He ended up performing memory feats for money.

Although his memory was overactive, S used it for some of the same reasons you use yours — to understand a language, find the way from place to place and develop skills, such as tying a shoelace and riding a bike. In short, having a memory means having a life.

Your Extraordinary "Ordinary" Memory

Publius Scipio, a general in ancient Rome, was able to recall the names of about 35 000 people. Although you might never be able to match his record, you have an amazing memory! Every day, it retrieves the masses of information you need: how to get out of bed, where to find your socks, what to eat for breakfast, when to go to school, who your teacher is, why the classroom buzzer rings, and on and on.

Your memory works surprisingly fast, too. Look at a sock and your mind whips through its "catalogue" of images, identifies the category the sock fits, comes up with a sound — a word — and you blurt out, "sock." All in 7/100 of a second! Not only does the word pop up, but you also remember what to do with a sock — stick it on your foot, not in the toaster.

Remarkably, you'll never have to worry about running out of room to store memories. If you stashed away 1000 new bits of info every second of your life, you'd still be using only part of your total storage space.

Your memory — that astonishing set of abilities to record and recall skills, events and knowledge — is very complex. How well it functions generally depends on you: your age, health, emotions and, especially, the way you store and use information. It's you who makes your memory tick.

- An aquarium octopus remembers the faces of its keepers, accepting food from some and squirting water at others.

Yoohoo!

Like most folks, you probably find faces easier to remember than names. When you meet someone, you might automatically focus on special facial features — eyes, nose, mouth and hair — that you're likely to recognize again. Your brain stores these images easily.

Names, however, are just words. You can't picture them, and they don't have much meaning — except for a few, such as Baker and White. Besides, different people may have the same name. That makes names tougher to store and recall. But the ones you use often can stick in your head almost as well as faces. One dogcare worker can rattle off the names of the 700 pets he looks after, but he seldom remembers what to call their owners.

The Memory Machine

When Henry M. of Connecticut awoke from surgery in 1953, his memory was shattered. Doctors had tried to cure his epilepsy — a disorder of the nervous system — by removing chunks of his brain. The operation improved his health, but it damaged his ability to form memories that lasted more than a few minutes. He would read the same story each day without recognizing it and forget someone he had met just moments earlier.

Henry still had scattered memories of the people, places and events he knew before his operation, and he could recall how to do things, such as eat, dress, talk, write and mow the lawn. He could even develop new skills, including tracing a star while looking in a mirror — but he couldn't remember ever having learned them.

Henry's life showed that remembering is not one ability, but several, and that different parts of the brain process or store different memories. While much about memory remains a mystery, studying Henry helped scientists develop some theories about where memories are stored and how they operate.

Cerebral cortex, or "gray matter"
This outer layer of the cerebrum receives messages from your senses and does most of your thinking. It stores your memories of facts and events, such as the names of different vegetables and the day you learned to ride a bicycle.

Cerebrum
Receives messages from your senses. Helps you learn and move.

Hippocampus
Located inside the brain, the hippocampus helps you store some memories for hours, weeks or years.

Brain stem
Controls your basic body functions, such as breathing and swallowing. Transfers messages between the nervous system and other parts of the brain.

Headquarters

Searching for a memory? Look no farther than your brain. That mass of soft cells inside your head isn't just one big blob. It has three main sections: brain stem, cerebrum (se-REE-brem) and cerebellum (ser-e-BELL-em). The cerebrum and cerebellum are the parts of the brain that scientists think are especially important for remembering.

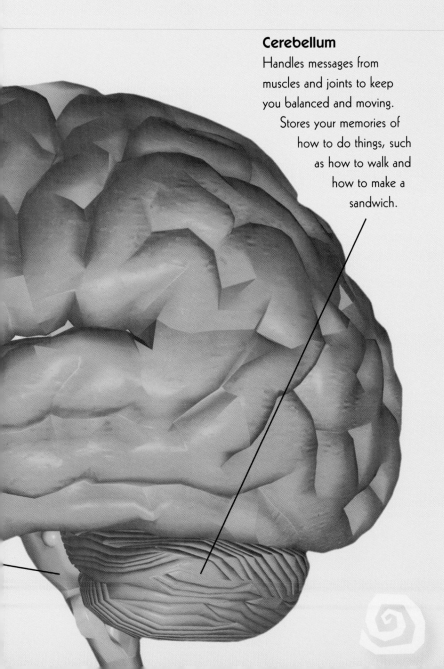

Cerebellum

Handles messages from muscles and joints to keep you balanced and moving. Stores your memories of how to do things, such as how to walk and how to make a sandwich.

Knowing the Enemy

Memory isn't all in your head. Throughout your body are white blood cells called lymphocytes (LIM-fo-sites) that have "memories," too. They remember which bacteria and viruses have attacked you and made you sick. If any of these enemies return, the lymphocytes react fast to destroy the invaders. A similar thing happens when you are vaccinated against diseases such as whooping cough and mumps. Weak or imitation bacteria or viruses are introduced to your body. Lymphocytes remember them, guarding you against an attack from real, full-strength enemies.

Tucking It Away

Back in the 1930s and 1940s, one scientist tried to discover just how important the cerebral cortex was to memory. He trained rats to run through a tricky maze, then removed some of the cerebral cortex from each rat. He figured that if memories were stored in the cortex, removing chunks of it should make remembering harder. However, the rats still found their way through the maze. Then the biologist removed more of the rats' cerebral cortex. Would they now forget their route through the maze? Surprisingly, they didn't. The biologist eventually gave up.

Today most scientists agree that memories are scattered — but organized. Take your memories of corn on the cob, for example. Scientists think that each memory sits near the part of the cerebral cortex where information from your senses first reaches your brain. Recollections of the smell and taste of corn settle in one area, while memories of its deep heat, yellow color and crunchy texture are stored in other parts. You might also call up related memories of corn roasts you've enjoyed, the corn-cob dolls your aunt crafted — even commercials for adhesives that help people eat corn on the cob without losing their false teeth. These are "what" memories — they help you recall what corn is like.

If you want to eat a cob of corn, you have to draw on memories from your cerebellum. This is where "how-to" information is stored. These memories tell you how to hold the cob of corn, open your mouth, bite and chew.

When you think of corn, your brain usually draws "what" and "how" memories together and organizes them into one grand memory, faster than you can blink an eye.

- When part of an event is familiar, your brain might occasionally fool you into thinking the whole event is familiar. You experience déjà vu — a creepy feeling that you're reliving something.

Seeing Memory

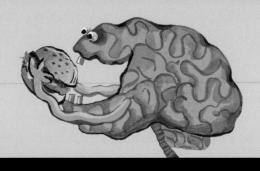

All the remembering your brain does makes it very hungry. That's why brain cells gobble up plenty of fuel — mostly oxygen and sugar. In fact, your brain burns 25 percent of all the oxygen you breathe in.

Scientists use the brain's hunger to discover more about where memory is stored. They "feed" brains by injecting volunteers with harmless chemicals that scanners can track. The parts of the brains that are thinking and remembering tend to "eat" the most and show up as colored spots on computer screens.

Shoe Size, Please

Suppose you're shopping for sneakers, and a store clerk asks for your shoe size. Just how do you retrieve it from your brain? Many scientists think that the memory of your shoe size may exist as a set of electrical signals that follow a particular path between your brain's nerve cells, called neurons. As you try to call the memory to mind, you trigger the signals, and they flash into action.

Your brain contains about 100 billion neurons that send and receive different signals. The neurons are so small that you would need a microscope to see one. Each has a body, a long tail — called an axon — and many short branches, or dendrites. The tail of one neuron almost touches the dendrites of another neuron — but not quite. Between any two neurons is a teeny gap.

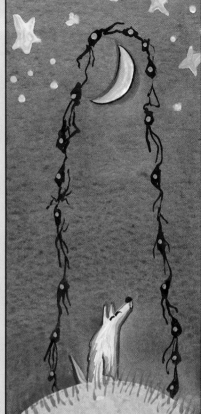

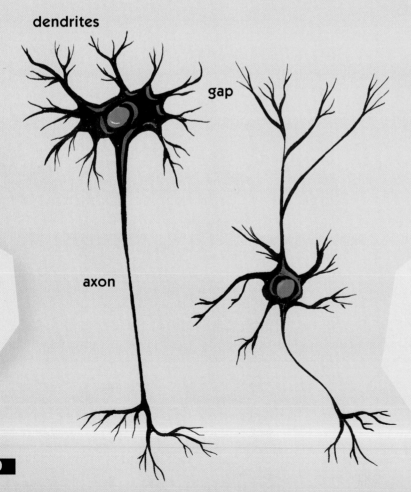

dendrites

gap

axon

- If all the neurons in your brain were strung end to end, they would reach to the moon and back.

- Your brain has about a trillion glial (GLEE-al) cells that supply nutrients to all your neurons and speed up their activity.

- Within a single second, your brain can send and receive millions of signals.

Here It Comes!

As you're about to tell the store clerk your sneaker size, an electrical signal zooms down an axon at speeds up to 320 km/h (200 m.p.h.). At the end of the axon, the signal sets off a shower of chemicals, called neurotransmitters. They cross the gap between neurons and stick to the dendrites of the next neuron. Some of these neurotransmitters set off another signal, which charges down the axon in that neuron — and on and on. Bingo! To your relief, you recall your shoe size almost instantly.

The action among the neurons is a little bit like kids playing with water pistols. When Sara showers Jeff's left arm (dendrites) with water (neurotransmitters), he uses his right hand (axon) to fire water at Justine's left arm (dendrites) and so on. The water (memory) travels around the group in no time.

Memory on the Menu?

If you don't know any words in Hungarian or Swahili, perhaps you could eat a memory that does. Sound like science fiction? During the 1950s and 1960s, some scientists thought memories were stored as molecules of protein — which could be eaten — and they tested their theory. They shone light on some flatworms, zapping them with electricity at the same time. The worms soon made the connection, shrinking in fear from the light even when they weren't getting zapped.

Then the scientists fed these worms to flatworms that had never been shocked. The new worms appeared to fear light, too, which seemed to support the theory of memory you could eat. Other scientists, however, had trouble getting the same results from similar experiments, and the theory died.

Remembering How and What

Big bones, small bones. Broken bones, solid bones. All uncovered by a hydraulic shovel at a city center construction site. The anthropologist called to examine the bones now sorts them in her lab. Expertly, she identifies each one—radius, ulna, humerus and so on. Bone by bone, she pieces together the remains of a human skeleton. An ancient one.

As she works, the anthropologist measures each bone, observing its condition and jotting the information on a clipboard by her side. Picturing another skeleton found in the city center last year, she thinks how similar it was —and writes that down, too.

Imagine how much harder this work would be if the anthropologist couldn't draw on her memory. In her mind, she stores images of bones — their size, shape, texture and the ways they all link together. She can use those images by matching them with the real bones in front of her. And that's not all.

Like you, the anthropologist draws on two main types of memory — procedural ("how" memory) and declarative ("what" memory). In her procedural memory are all the skills she's learned, such as measuring bones and writing notes. Her declarative memory contains memories of things. These may be events, such as her examination of the skeleton found last year, or other types of information — the many facts, figures and words she knows.

• Trained elephants can remember the meanings of about 100 different commands, such as "wash behind your ears."

Your "How" Memory

When you walk, you don't consciously have to recall how to keep your balance or move your feet. You just do it. Walking is a set of skills you've been practicing since you were a baby, and now it's automatic. That's why you can walk and talk at the same time. Like many other skills, walking is tucked away as part of your "how," or procedural, memory.

Along with well-practiced skills, your procedural memory includes information on how to sense things. For instance, your brain knows how to guide your hand so that it can feel for some coins in your pocket. You can not only walk and talk at the same time, but also grab change for the bus.

Wait for meee!

You Try It

Add mirror-tracing to your memory bank of skills. Draw a large five-pointed star on a sheet of paper (don't worry about making the lines straight or even). Now lay it on a tabletop in front of a large mirror. Using ink of a different color, trace the star you drew by looking only in the mirror. Feel awkward? Sure, but if you try again every day, it gets much easier. Keep track of the number of times you have to trace the star before you can do it without hesitating.

Your "What" Memory

Remember your first day at school? Know the capital city of France? Both these things — an event and a fact — are kept in your "what," or declarative, memory. It stores two main types of information: memories of events from your personal past and all the words, facts and figures you know.

Event memories are usually easy to retrieve because they're meaningful to you. They often come to mind as whole bundles of connected memories. Besides an event — a thrilling ride on a rollercoaster, perhaps — you'll likely also recall the place where it occurred. You'll "see" the scene in color, "hear" the sounds of people shrieking and "smell" the hot dogs and popcorn. And you'll certainly remember the queasy — but excited — way you felt at the time. All these memories will rise together in your head like a scene from a play.

• Scientists think that only mammals and birds can have memories of events.

Stashing Facts

The rest of the information in your "what" memory forms your own personal encyclopedia and dictionary of words, facts and figures. These memories include your address, the names of your friends, the differences between apples and pumpkins, and the distance around Earth.

Your brain seems to sort words in your declarative memory into about 20 groups, including one group for animals and another for vegetables and fruits. To put words together in sentences, you likely use your "how," or procedural, memory. It strings the words in the right order. If it didn't, you might write a sentence like this: cow The moon over jumped the.

Memories can affect your behavior in funny ways. You can see this this by asking a friend to say some words that you will spell to her. Then spell out "mackay," "macdonald" and "macduff." Talk about something else for a few minutes, then spell out "machinery" and ask your friend to say it. Did she say "mac-hinery" instead of "machinery"?

Repeat the same experiment with a different friend and use these words: "tractor," "bulldozer," "chainsaw." After a break, spell "machinery" and ask your friend to pronounce it. Why would you be surprised if he said "mac-hinery"?

The Short...

Memories of "how" or "what" are like money. You can save them for a short time, a long time or almost any amount of time in between.

Try a different dance step ("how" memory) or visit your cousin's new house ("what" memory), and the step or visit might stay in your short-term memory for just a few seconds or minutes. Short-term memory can temporarily store up to seven things at a time — enough to hang on to a seven-digit phone number until you dial it. But if you didn't keep thinking about it, the number would disappear.

However, some scientists believe that short-term memory stores even more. They prefer to call it "working memory" and think it includes the quick links you make with the stuff you've already stashed away. For instance, your working memory might recall similarities between the new dance step and another one that you already know. Or it might remember that your friend lives on the same street as your cousin. A working memory also makes it possible for you to do two things at a time. Without it, you might not be able to hum while you dance.

... and the Long of It

Practice the new dance step or visit your cousin's new house several times, and you move the memory from short-term to long-term storage. Repetition is one way to make the shift. Memories can sit in long-term storage for hours, weeks, years — perhaps a lifetime. Your brain's hippocampus helps choose where these facts and events are stored.

Your brain actually changes as it transfers short-term memories to long-term storage. It produces fresh dendrites, forming stronger connections between neurons so that the memories stay with you longer. It also strengthens the links between existing dendrites and axons. Generally, the older the memories and the more they're recalled, the better they stick.

What happens to the short-term memories that don't move into long-term storage? They simply disappear.

- By about the time you turn eight, your ability to use your short-term memory is well developed.

- Even bees remember some things. Once trained to link food with blue-colored mats, bees still head for blue mats — set among gray, black and white ones — several months later.

You Try It

Put your short-term memory to work. Have someone write down a seven-digit number. Read it twice, cover it up and breathe in and out a few times. Then write down the number. Did you remember it correctly?

Now transfer the same number to long-term memory. Say it and write it out until you think you have it memorized. Do something else for an hour. Do you still remember the number? If it stuck, give yourself a pat on the head. Your brain has just sprouted new dendrites.

Ever-Changing Memories

You're standing on a street corner when — bang! — two cars collide right in front of you. The police arrive and ask you questions about what you saw. You remember it all, exactly ... or do you?

In one study, two groups of volunteers watched a film of a car accident. Researchers asked the first group how fast they thought the cars were going before they HIT. They asked the second group how fast they thought the cars were going before they SMASHED. A week later, 14 percent of the first group and 32 percent of the second group "remembered" seeing shattered glass around the cars. But there wasn't any. The stronger word, "smashed," seemed to suggest greater car damage than "hit" and altered more memories.

Studies show that memories can change — even in the calm of a research lab. Out in the real world, eyewitnesses often have more trouble recalling events accurately. People who witness crimes can incorrectly remember important details, such as the gender and race of the criminals. Their memories can also be altered by some of the questions police officers ask them.

Repainting the Past

Even memories of everyday events are not exact records. They're a bit different each time you call them to mind. They change according to the new information you store away, events occurring in your life, plus the actions and spoken memories of other people. If you once feared being sucked down the bathtub drain, for instance, you might not recall how truly terrified you were — you've since learned that drains don't suck kids. But your changing memories are usually similar enough to the actual events that you're not aware of the differences.

As you grow and mature, your memories evolve in the same ways you do. Your attitudes and beliefs color what you remember as you look back on your life. In fact, some people completely forget pieces of the past that no longer fit the images they have of themselves. Happy adults who had troubled childhoods tend to block out many of their hard times. Without realizing it, they might also create new, happier "childhood memories."

- In North America, about half the people convicted of crimes who were later found to be innocent were condemned because of the mistaken memories of eyewitnesses.

- Like everyone else, you "adopt" memories. You might have heard stories about yourself as a toddler so often that you think you remember them, too.

Set up an eyewitness experiment by inviting some friends to watch you "commit a crime." While they are waiting, leave the room and change your clothes. You might also want to add a hat, scarf, sunglasses and gloves. Then race into the room where your friends are, grab an object and run out — fast.

After you've changed back into your first set of clothes, question each friend separately. Ask what was stolen and what the robber was wearing. Throw in a trick question to see how you might alter their memories. For instance, ask what was sticking out of the robber's back pocket — even though nothing was.

Drawing a Blank

English physicist and mathematician Sir Isaac Newton (1642–1727) was one of the world's most brilliant scientists. He was also forgetful. Newton spent so much time thinking about his work that he had trouble remembering everyday matters. He often lost track of time, sometimes forgetting to sleep or eat. His cat grew fat on the dinners that Newton — and his memory — left sitting on the table.

You don't need to be a great scientist to have a lot on your mind. Everybody experiences "information overload" now and then, and some things are forgotten. That's normal. So is being stuck for a word. "Igloo," for instance, may not spring to mind when you're thinking of a round house made of ice. Psychologists call this kind of forgetting a "tip-of-the-tongue" event because what you're trying to say seems so close. You might recall the first letter or number of syllables in the word. Usually it occurs to you after a minute or two. Your age, lifestyle, emotions and the way you apply your mind — or don't — also affect your memory.

Hmmm?

- On average, people forget about 99 bits of information out of every 100 they receive.

- Young children observe and remember more details than most adults do. Forgetting what's not useful is something people have to learn.

Filtering Details

Picture your favorite pair of sneakers. Do you remember what colors appear on the tops — and bottoms? The number of holes the laces pass through? The pattern on the rubber soles? Maybe not, but that's fine. Unless you need all that detail, there's no point littering your mind with it.

You regularly ignore a lot of information — the kinds of trees in the school yard and the number of freckles on your nose. Like most people, you block out what you find unimportant or uninteresting. Scientists call that "perceptual filtering." You usually remember just enough about an object to be able to recognize it. And when you remember events, you mentally record only the most significant details. In fact, being able to forget what you don't need helps you make sense of the world.

What's considered useful or important varies from person to person, and from time to time. For example, if you end up repairing shoes for a living, you'll probably pay greater attention to sneakers than you do now.

Remember me?

You've seen a nickel thousands of times, and you can easily recognize one at a glance. Try drawing a nickel from memory — both sides of it. Then compare your drawings with a real nickel. If you left out several details, you're like most people. Ask your friends to do the same thing and compare results. Then find someone who collects coins and have that person draw a nickel from memory. Would you expect a coin collector to remember more details than you did?

Acting Your Age

It's not surprising that you can't remember much of your life before you turned four. At birth, your brain was packed with neurons, but not all parts were operating fully. And the memories you had as a baby and a toddler were likely poorly stored in the first place.

You'll also have some problems remembering things when you're old. As you age, bits of protein gradually clog the gaps between neurons. Tucking away new information and calling it quickly to mind again will become more challenging.

At any age, there's little difference between the memories of females and males — except when people try to find their way around. Females seem to have more trouble remembering long routes, but they're often better than males at recalling the landmarks they pass.

- Saying no to veggies and fruits can be bad for your memory. Many plant foods reduce cell damage in the brain.

- Poisonous fumes in an underground mine caused one man to forget his second language, German. After a short rest outside the mine, his language skills returned.

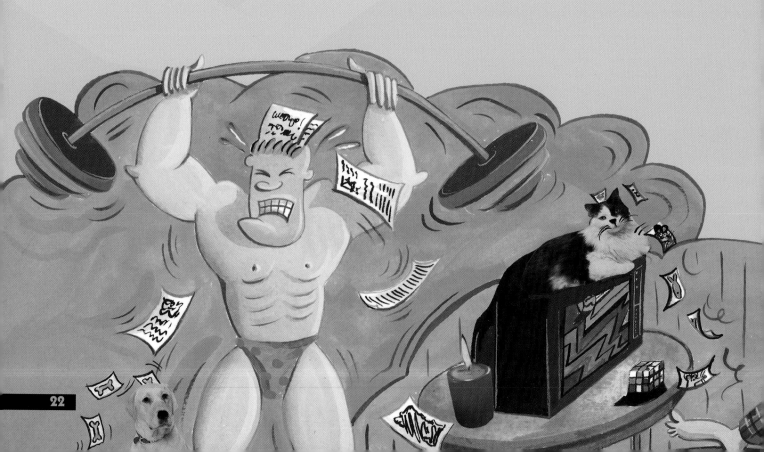

Sick and Tired

Skimp on sleep, stop exercising or eat poorly and you may have a tough time remembering. Do all three at once and you can't expect much at all from your brain.

When you're tired, it's difficult to pay attention and store what you want to remember. It's also brain-draining to recall the info you stashed away earlier. Some scientists think sleep may actually help your memory. You may fix facts and skills more firmly in your mind during the dream stages of your sleep.

Lack of exercise leaves you weaker mentally as well as physically. Studies show that people who spend a lot of time sitting around do worse on memory tests than those who work out regularly. Exercise helps to pump plenty of oxygen-rich blood to the brain.

Meals that don't provide the nutrition you need also weaken your memory. For instance, too little glucose — a sugar found in both plants and animals — threatens the levels of acetylcholine (a-set-el-KO-leen) in your brain. This neurotransmitter helps signals leap from neuron to neuron. Glucose is especially important at the start of each day, when your brain is starving after a night without food. But don't overdo it. Big meals can make you groggy and slow your mental processes. And drinking too much caffeine, in coffee, tea or soft drinks, can disturb your night's rest — and your memory.

The Shrinking Brain

Over time, people whose diets lack vitamin B1 (thiamine) risk developing a frightening disorder called Korsakoff's syndrome. Named after the Russian psychiatrist who first described it in 1887, this disorder can cause its victims' brains to shrink. The memory loss is huge, especially for events in the recent past. Simple memories — where they went that morning and the person they just saw — vanish completely.

So remember! Eat your vitamin B1, which is found in foods such as grains, peas and beans.

Forget It!

Bah, humbug! Negative moods and emotions can affect how you log something in your memory — and how you call it back. That's why it's not a good idea to study when you're mad or feeling blue. Anger and depression make concentrating difficult, which in turn hampers your memory. Depression also robs your enthusiasm for most things, making them harder to remember. You'd be much smarter to work when you're cheerful.

Fear and shock also affect memory. A really frightening event is usually easy to recall, but one that's mildly disturbing can be tough to remember. Your mind may try to shut out unpleasant memories.

Stress often gets in the way of memory. It can cause your adrenal glands to release a hormone called cortisol, which reduces the amount of glucose your brain neurons can absorb. Underfed neurons don't perform well.

- Presented with 64 feeding tubes in a lab, hummingbirds remembered — better than the researchers — which 32 tubes contained food.

- Folks often forget who told them a certain joke. That's why they may end up telling the same joke to the person they first heard it from.

More Memory Busters

Memory and muscles are somewhat alike. Neglect them and they shrivel — fast. Unless you make an effort to recall and use what you are learning, you can lose more than half of it within 30 minutes. The rest gradually fades away.

Facts and events that are similar are especially easy to forget. They tend to blend together. You may remember a lot about the first day of this school year — even what you wore, who you talked with and how you felt. But the details of your fourth, nineteenth or thirty-third school day likely escape you — unless something made them special.

New skills and information sometimes interfere with what you stored earlier. Suppose you're memorizing a poem. You should allow about six hours for it to sink in to your memory. If you try to remember another poem in that same six-hour period, you might forget the first one.

From time to time, you'll want to replace old information with new, up-to-date stuff. That's usually easy to do. Change your address or your locker combination, and the previous one soon dims in your memory.

Interfere with someone's memory. Get together with two friends and ask Friend A to name the titles of seven movies. Ask Friend B to recite the list by heart (order doesn't matter). Then name seven other movie titles and ask Friend B to repeat the first list. Did your interference make the job any tougher?

Who Am I?

A character in a movie tumbles from her speeding horse, strikes her head on a rock and spends the rest of her life wondering who she is. That's amnesia (am-NEE-zha) — in the movies. In real life, this form of memory loss is much more complex. It's true that physical injury to the brain is the most common cause, but illnesses and brain tumors can also trigger amnesia. And there's more than one kind.

People with retrograde amnesia have trouble remembering what happened BEFORE their injury — especially during the most recent hours, weeks, months or years.

But they might recall old events well and have no problem forming new memories of things that occurred after the injury.

Anterograde amnesia leaves people unable to remember events that happened AFTER their injury. Their memories of life before the injury may be quite clear. However, like people who have Korsakoff's syndrome (see page 23), they have trouble forming new long-term memories.

A third kind — global transitory amnesia — usually doesn't last long, but it can affect memories of events both before AND after an injury.

Who am I?

Fading Away

Any illness limits memory — at least for a short while. When you're sick, you don't pay close attention to things, so you don't do a good job of storing facts. Diseases that damage the brain can cause more serious memory problems. Alzheimer's (ALTS-hi-merz) disease, for instance, is a brain disorder that mostly affects declarative ("what") memory. People who suffer from this illness gradually lose their recollections of the events that made up their lives. Their storehouse of general information also slips away.

Parkinson's and Huntington's diseases are two other brain disorders that affect memory in tragic ways. But unlike victims of Alzheimer's, people who have these illnesses lose their procedural ("how") memory, bit by bit.

Stroke patients with extensive brain damage can suffer a complete loss of language. They can't understand what is said to them or recall how to read, write or speak. Stroke patients with milder brain damage may lose only some or part of these skills.

Woof!

- **It's possible to lose the ability to recognize music, while still being able to identify other sounds, such as talking, barking and honking.**

- **The sense of smell in people with Alzheimer's disease often dwindles along with their memory.**

Doogie Mouse

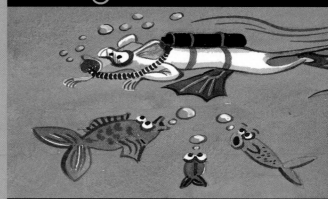

Meet Doogie, super mouse. In a research lab, it can remember where to find an underwater platform, recognize a building block it found earlier and watch out for signs that it's about to get an electric shock. Doogie learns faster and remembers longer than the average mouse because scientists have tinkered with its brain. They boosted the ability of its neurons to form memories.

What scientists learn from Doogie might apply to humans. Patients who have memory-killing diseases, such as Alzheimer's, might respond well to a similar technique.

Sharpening Your Memory

Disaster struck a banquet hall in Greece around 500 B.C. — the roof fell in, killing all the guests. The only survivor was the dinnertime entertainer — a poet named Simonides (si-MAHN-a-deez). Relatives rushed to the rubble to claim the bodies, but the victims had been crushed beyond recognition. Simonides solved the problem by recalling the exact seating arrangement around the table — guest by guest.

The experience helped Simonides realize that storing facts in an organized way makes them easier to remember. He became the "father" of mnemonic (nee-MON-ik) techniques — methods of sharpening memory. Over the centuries, people developed many mnemonics, such as linking facts with places, making up rhymes and stories, and playing number games. Using these techniques can help you recall specific facts — even though they won't improve your memory in general.

Order, Order

If the thousands of books in a library were just tossed in a room, you'd need months to uncover what you wanted. Organizing them in a logical way makes it much easier to find a specific book. That also applies to facts stored in your memory.

You don't have any shelves in your head, but you can use mental frameworks to help organize and retrieve information. For instance, it's easier to remember who's in your class if you note who is sitting where. Later, you can retrieve their names by picturing each row in the classroom.

One of the oldest mnemonic techniques, designed by Simonides, is called the method of loci (LOW-kigh). It uses a mental framework to help you recall lists of things in order. First, build the framework by thinking of familiar places — along your street, perhaps. Next, picture each place with an item from one of your lists. Then mentally "visit" the places in order and name the items you "see." To remember all the mayors of your town, for example, you might imagine Ms. Neely on your front lawn and Mr. Collins strolling down the sidewalk. If you make your mental pictures big, colorful — even funny — they're easier to recall. So you might picture Ms. Neely kneeling and Mr. Collins walking like a collie.

You Try It

Use the method of loci to remember seven things you must do in order. First, think of seven places in your house, such as the coat closet, hallway and living room. Imagine starting from the front of the house and walking to each of these places in a particular order. Repeat this "walk" several times.

Now ask someone to give you seven tasks, such as watering the daisies, walking the dog and mailing a letter. Imagine doing one task in each of your seven places. Can you see yourself watering a giant daisy in the coat closet? Use your memory to list the jobs in order by mentally walking through your house.

- Memory-improving mnemonic techniques were named after Mnemosyne (nee-MOSS-e-nee), the Greek goddess of memory, who was believed to know everything.

- In 1974, a citizen of Yangon, Myanmar (formerly Burma), recited 16 000 pages of religious text by memory.

Whiff of Memory

Organized or not, information is more likely to stick in your head if you link it with your senses. Especially smell. The part of the brain that receives odor signals from your nose sits close to where many of your memories are stored. Link a fact with a scent and the odor will help you remember it. In one study, people who smelled butterscotch and peppermint while learning a word list remembered the words best whenever those smells were present.

The more senses you link with information — even just in your imagination — the easier you'll recall it. So go wild with your homework. To remember that Alexander Graham Bell invented the telephone, try "seeing" an A-shaped phone with a giant bell and a big graham wafer on top. "Hear" the bell ring. "Feel" the vibrations. "Smell" and "taste" the graham wafer as you answer the phone.

- Amazing! Your brain can remember up to 10 000 different smells.

- Smells are easily linked with emotions. Remember an odor — even unconsciously — and it can trigger the same feelings you had the first time you smelled it.

Now, what *was* that guy's name?

Lime for a Dime

If you had lived in Europe centuries ago, you would have heard rhymes every day. People used them to remember all kinds of things. French merchants, for example, depended on a set of 137 two-line poems to recall the business arithmetic they needed.

Rhymes are still used as mnemonics. Similar sounding words are easy for minds to link. "One, two, buckle my shoe/Three, four, knock at the door ..." helps a young child recall numbers in order. And "Columbus sailed the ocean blue/In fourteen hundred ninety-two" is a good rhyme for making a bit of history cling to your brain.

Other mnemonics use words formed from the first letter of each word in a group. NATO is much simpler to fix in your memory than North Atlantic Treaty Organization. And Roy G. Biv helps you remember the colors in a rainbow: red, orange, yellow, green, blue, indigo and violet.

Storytelling helps memory, too. You can use it to order your thoughts or jog your brain with your senses. So don't get stumped naming the countries of South America. Make up a story about Big Brazil with his twins, Paraguay and Uruguay, who were shivering in Chile when along came ...

To remember people's names, try rhyming them with their personalities, looks or hobbies. It's easier to do if you shorten the names—using Liz instead of Elizabeth, for instance. And remember, you're just trying to create a fun rhyme, not great poetry. In fact, the zanier the rhyme, the easier it is to recall. How could you forget a good-looking guy called Jason if you thought of him as Jas the face? Or what about fun-loving Ashley? Ash, what a bash!

Playing with Numbers

Many people find numbers especially difficult to remember. Others rattle them off without even trying. Gon Yangling of China, for instance, could recite 15 000 phone numbers by heart!

Mnemonic techniques that can help you recall numbers often use codes. To remember a long number, you could pair the digits 0 to 9 with a series of words that are related: 0 = cheek, 1 = eye ... 6 = nose ... 9 = chin. Or use words that rhyme with the digits they represent: 0 = hero, 1 = sun ... 6 = kicks ... 9 = pine. So the year that people first walked on the moon — 1969 — would be sun, pine, kicks, pine. To make it memorable, turn it into a picture story: the sun (1) is shining on two pines (two 9s). Between the pines, a donkey kicks (6) a man to the moon. Goofy stories are usually easy to remember.

Long figures, such as the distance to the moon, can be broken into groups of four or five numbers, coded, then linked together in a story.

Memory Workout

Want to remember a good joke, today's history lesson or the fastest way to type? Here's a tip that can help: repeat, repeat, repeat. Repetition helps keep memories strong, but be sure to give your brain a break from time to time. Spend no more than an hour learning or practicing, then do something else for a few minutes. The change will help anchor the info in your mind.

Repetition not only improves your "how" memory for skills and your "what" memory for words, facts and figures, but it also speeds up your recall. Even if you give up typing or don't tell your joke for years, all that repeating can make it easier to relearn later.

One warning: repetition can confuse your "what" memory of events. If you spend all your summers at the same lake, your memories of those times tend to blend together. It's easier to recall a particular summer day if you can connect it with something unusual — the memory of a raccoon stealing your picnic lunch or the gigantic fish you caught.

- **Some people have amazing memories for only one type of information — the populations of cities, for example.**

You Try It

Give your memory a workout by memorizing a fun poem by an unknown author. Read "Animal Fair" twice, then copy it down twice. After a short break, read the poem again. Can you write it out by memory? If not, read it and write it until it sticks in your head. Can you recite the poem a day, a week or a month later?

Animal Fair

I went to the animal fair,
The birds and beasts were there.
The big baboon, by the light of the moon,
Was combing his auburn hair.
The monkey, he got drunk,
And sat on the elephant's trunk.
The elephant sneezed and fell on his knees,
And what became of the monk, the monk?

Recreating the Scene

Suppose you've searched the house, but you can't find your change purse. Don't panic. Just think when and where you last saw it. Picture what you were doing then, even what you were smelling or hearing. Oh, yes ... you had just finished dressing and could smell breakfast cooking. You picked up your change purse from the dresser and ... the hall phone rang. It was Uncle Fred with a message for your dad. Hmm, no pen handy. You raced to the kitchen and dug through the junk drawer to find a pen. That's it! You must have set down your change purse in the drawer!

People can remember things more easily by recalling—or revisiting—the scene connected with them. In one study, volunteers in a basement room were asked to memorize a list of words and were tested on their recall. When they were retested on a different floor, their scores dropped. The volunteers were then told to picture the basement as they took the test again. Their scores improved—but not as much as when they returned to the basement for yet another test.

- Police officers sometimes ask volunteers to reenact a crime, hoping to jog the memory of a witness.

- If you see a movie when you're cranky, you'll likely remember it best when you're in a cranky mood.

Setting up Reminders

Writing weakens the memory — according to ancient Greek philosophers, such as Plato. They feared that writing things down would replace mental exercise, making people very forgetful. But modern life is so busy and fast-paced that most people's memories can use a bit of help. Think of all the telephone messages that would be forgotten if there was no way to jot them down. Writing shopping lists or marking birthdays on calendars makes them easier to remember.

You can create other kinds of reminders, too. For instance, you can remind yourself to take something with you when you go out by putting it in your way. If you lean your umbrella against the door, you're sure to grab it as you go.

Find special hideaways for things you seem to misplace easily. Your pen, for example. Choose some unusual spot that will stay in your mind — on the top of a picture frame or on the base of a lamp. Put your pen back there whenever you're through with it.

If you have a number of things to do, try setting out reminders before you begin. Stand the broom by the toilet, put the bag of dog food on the floor and lay out the placemats. Then it's easy to remember that you have to sweep the bathroom, feed Fluffy and set the table.

Memory Theaters

Several hundred years ago, Europeans created some of the most elaborate mind-joggers ever — wooden "dollhouses," called memory theaters. Large and fancy, each of these theaters contained several rooms and many cubbyholes. People "stored" their memories by linking each one with a specific spot. They later brought these memories to mind just by looking through the miniature house.

One of the most well-known memory theaters was designed in Italy during the 1500s by a man named Giulio Camillo. The model was big enough to hold two people and — according to Camillo — every memory that a person could have. Featuring several passages and stairways, masses of little drawers and many carved emblems, the theater took Camillo most of his life to create.

Memories Are You

The tohunga were powerful guardians — not of lives, but of memories. Century after century, they kept track of the history of their people, the Maori of New Zealand. The tohunga told stories of Maori ancestors, who came by canoe from Eastern Polynesia. They described traditional travel routes and important events. Since the Maori had no written language, the tohunga committed their history to memory, along with their knowledge of skills, such as carving and canoe-building. They passed all this on from generation to generation.

Like the Maori, many early peoples depended on official history-keepers with excellent memories. The Irish had their shanachie and the Greeks, their mnemons. They were all highly respected because they provided a service people valued.

Today most societies depend on written records, but we still treasure our shared, or collective, memories as much as ever. Combined with your own recollections, collective memories help define the world you live in, the person you are and the future you hold.

Memories Are Us

No two people have the same set of memories, but many recollections overlap. For instance, everyone in town recalls the hockey game that put a local team in the national finals and the violent windstorm that ripped roofs off houses. Collective memories — good and bad — draw individuals together, making them feel they're one.

People in small groups — families, clubs, neighborhoods and villages — experience many of the same events and build up a large bank of shared memories. But even folks who live far apart share experiences that give them memories in common. Members of the same religion, for instance, take part in similar rituals and ceremonies worldwide.

Collective memories have the power to change lives. They can provoke rebellions, renew national pride and strengthen values. When people recall slavery, for instance, they treasure freedom even more.

The flip side of collective remembering is social "amnesia," or collective forgetting. It can weaken a sense of identity and destroy bonds of loyalty. The Etruscans, who ruled Italy from 1100 B.C. to 400 B.C., lost an important part of themselves when their long history virtually disappeared. It vanished with their memory-keepers when Romans invaded and took over the country.

Lest We Forget

The flags are lowered, the poppy wreaths laid. With heads bowed in silence, people around the world honor the memory of men and women who served their nations in war.

Some countries hold war memorial services every November 11 — the day in 1918 when an agreement brought World War I to an end. Called Remembrance Day in Canada, Veterans Day in the United States and Jour du Souvenir in France, this special day focuses on battles past and lives lost. It also draws people together, uniting them in their hope for world peace.

You and Your Memory Bank

Lose your personal memories and you lose yourself — where you've been, who you know, what you care about. Everything that is uniquely you is gone.

Think of Henry M., the man whose brain operation stole his ability to make new memories. When he glanced in a mirror, he couldn't even recognize himself. The face he remembered was a young man's — the face that had been his years before his surgery.

Much of what you've tucked away in your memory bank is essential, but not earthshaking — how to open a door or tell a car from a cow. Remembering words of praise and hugs of appreciation, however, helps to shape your mental image of yourself. Who you are grows out of your past — as you recall it. Day by day, you are what you remember.

Memory for Tomorrow

Want to know what you did 4 hours and 15 minutes ago? How about the third morning of last month at exactly 9:30? Get out the gadgets and you can keep track of everything you do. Miniaturized computer and camcorder technology have joined forces to record lives moment by moment. Just attach a gizmo and switch it on.

But why? Who needs or wants all that data? How meaningful would it be to you — or anyone else — five or ten years from now? Ancient memory-keepers were much choosier about what they hung onto, and they let their stories evolve, like the memory processes in your head. They made memories relevant to their listeners over the years.

Rather than trying to record more and more, you might prefer to make better use of your memories. Scientists have discovered that the neurons in your head react to one another — not just to the sensations that enter your brain. Like an artist mixing colors, you can link and blend signals to create new ones. So tap into your creativity. Gather up your memories — both personal and collective — and let your imagination take flight.

- At age 16, Edward Robb Ellis of New York started a diary. By the time he turned 70, his journal contained about 15 million words. Now that's a lot of memories.

- Japan's Yoshiro NakaMats — who has patented more than 2000 inventions — credits his memory storehouse with freeing his mind to be creative.

You Try It

Discover what memories your mind chooses to hold and how they change over time. At the end of one fun-packed Saturday, jot down the details of your day: where you went, what you did and saw, who you spoke with, how you felt and so on. The more details you include, the better. Put the date on your paper and store it somewhere safe.

After periods of a week, a month, six months and a year, describe the same day again — without looking at your earlier notes. Each time, include all the detail you can, then date and store your writing. After a year, compare your five descriptions. How did they change?

Index